40 Stories to Stir the Soul

JOAN CHITTISTER

Benetvision
Erie, Pennsylvania

$6.00
Quantity discounts available.

355 East Ninth Street
Erie, PA 16503-1107

Phone: 814-459-5994   Fax: 814-459-8066
benetvision@benetvision.org
www.joanchittister.org

Benetvision exists to encourage the development of contemporary spirituality from a feminist, global and monastic perspective through the works of Joan Chittister.

Cover photo by Carolyn Gorny-Kopkowski,OSB

ISBN: 978 1-890890-24-3

10 11 12 13 4 3 2 1

Table of Contents

Make your own private Holy Week Retreat.

In the space provided at the end of each chapter, paste a photo... clip an article...copy a quote or poem...draw...write a word, phrase or poem that reflects the theme.

Introduction

"God made human beings because God loved stories," Rabbi Nachman wrote.

And we, who are made in God's image and likeness, love stories, too.
Who doesn't hold in their storehouse of memories
    stories learned in a mother's arms,
    stories told at family gatherings,
    stories heard in church or temple, stories that shape a lifeline?

Those of you who follow Joan Chittister's writings know that she loves stories.
    She loves soul-size stories, the kind that you tell and never tire of retelling.
    She loves stories that pave a pathway to meaning and purpose.
    She loves stories that light candles in the dark recesses of the heart.
    She loves stories that you can play with, pulling apart each word and idea with abandon.
    She loves stories from every religious tradition—all the tales, the sayings, the myths, the fables, the proverbs and the parables.

Joan Chittister knows that we learn best by stories.

A good story is a treasure worth selling all one owns to possess.
It can shake us by the roots, make us rethink old truths, paste large questions in our sky, inspire us to reach for what we cannot.

This book is proof that stories do that for Joan Chittister.

The Jewish tradition teaches that the shortest distance between a human being and God is through a story. Let's see if that's true.

—Mary Lou Kownacki, editor

Beauty

There was a special prison In Uruguay for political prisoners. Here they were not allowed to talk without permission or whistle, smile, sing, walk fast, or greet other prisoners; nor could they make or receive drawings of pregnant women, couples, butterflies, stars or birds. One Sunday afternoon, Didako Perez, a school teacher who was tortured and jailed "for having ideological ideas," is visited by his five-year-old daughter Milay. She brings him a drawing of birds. The guards destroy it at the entrance of the jail.

On the following Sunday, Milay brings him a drawing of trees. Trees are not forbidden, and the drawing gets through. Her father praises her work and asks about the colored circles scattered in the treetops, many small circles half-hidden among the branches: "Are they oranges? What fruit is it?" The child puts her finger to her mouth, "Shh."

And she whispers in her father's ear, "Don't you see they are eyes? They're the eyes of the birds that I've smuggled in for you."

–Eduardo Galeano

BEAUTY, WE'RE TOLD, is a basic human instinct, the kind of thing that separates us from the animals, a kind of intrinsic quality of the human soul, the irrepressible expression of contemplative insight. It has something to do with what it means to be alive. But is this true? And how do we know that?

I remember being shocked into a new sense of what it means to be human in an inhuman environment in the worst slum in Haiti. Here people live in one room hovels made of corrugated steel over mud floors. They bear and raise one child after another here. They eat the leftovers of society. They scrounge for wood to cook with. They sleep in filth and live in rags and barely smile and cannot read. But in the middle of such human degradation they paint bright colors and brilliant scenes of a laughing, loving, wholesome community. They carve faces. They paint strident colors on bowls made out of coconuts. They play singing drums across the bare mountains that raise the cry of the human heart. They manufacture beauty in defiance of what it means to live an ugly, forgotten life on the fringe of the United States, the wealthiest nation the world has ever known. They are a sign that a society that can make such beauty is capable of endless human potential, however much struggle it takes to come to fullness. They are a sign of possibility and aspiration and humanity that no amount of huts or guns or poverty or starvation can ever squelch.

See instructions for this space on page 4.

God has made everything beautiful in its time.
Ecclesiastes 3:11

Being Imperfect

The Talmud tells of an old man in the village who kept giving money to ne'er-do-wells. The villagers were aghast at such wantonness. "Why give these people money when you know they'll only waste it?" they wanted to know. And the old man answered, "Shall I be pickier with them than God has been with me?"

I RAN THROUGH the pane glass front of a candy store when I was ten years old. Besides the fact that I was not to be in that particular store at that particular time, it was an added expense that my parents could not really afford at the time. I sat on the living room floor all day long waiting for my father to come home and punish me. But all he said was, "Are you hurt? No? Then good, what did you learn from it?" I didn't "merit" that love.

And I have an idea that someplace along the line, even you have managed to escape the just desert of your actions. In fact, we'd all be somewhere else right now if God were a God of arithmetic. None of us have perfect scores. All of us have been saved from ourselves and through no merit of our own.

And that's the problem: If we have to merit heaven, we're never going to get it. Because we can't. We aren't made to be perfect; we're made to be us. We're made to grow slowly. We're made to begin again and again and again. We're made to demonstrate God's justice and exercise God's mercy, both of which are clearly different from our own.

See instructions for this space on page 4.

The reign of God is at hand.
Matthew 3:2

Being Myself

Before he died, Rabbi Zusya of Hanipol said, "In the world to come, they will not ask me, 'Why were you not Moses?' They will ask me, 'Why were you not Zusya?'"

IMAGE-MAKING is a growth industry these days. Someone, somewhere tells us how to "dress for success." For a small fee, they will create résumés for us out of nothing. They give workshops that create for us, in six easy lessons or less, the kind of McPeople society that makes us all wonder what we're really seeing when we look at someone.

It's not that dressing for the occasion, speaking clearly, and learning how to define ourselves are not important skills. But learning how to present myself so people can see at a glance the kind of person I really am down deep and learning how to make who I really am invisible are two different things.

When who we make people think we are has become our defense against who we truly are, we are about as far away from the ancient meaning of humility, the fine art of being ourselves, as it is possible to get. Then it is not the jewelry we wear that is fake. It is we ourselves who are false.

See instructions for this space on page 4.

You are precious in my eyes,
you are honored and I love you.
Isaiah 43:4

Celebration

Once a little village received word that a great wise man was coming to visit. The wise man, or zaddick, had promised to answer any question the people might have about God. They were greatly honored by the visit, but as time passed, a curious anxiety began to overtake them. The only question they could think of was: "What kind of question do we ask a zaddick?"

When the day of the zaddick's visit arrived, the people were so upset they couldn't think or speak at all. They sat in mortified silence, as an old and bearded man in tattered coat walked in calmly and took his place in front of them. The silence continued. The mortification increased. The zaddick waited patiently, but no one even dared look at him.

The zaddick cast an eye about the crowd. One of his eyebrows raised, and a faint smile played about his mouth. He began to hum, quietly at first but then with increasing vigor. One of his feet began to tap a rhythm on the floor; and suddenly, as if there were no stopping it, his voice broke into song.

The people forgot themselves as the joy of the zaddick flowed into them. They began to sing along with him; and before they knew it, they were up and dancing. They sang and danced to God, and about God, and with God—on and on until nothing but the joy of God had any meaning.

The wise man clapped his hands for them to stop and said, "I trust this answers your question?"

WORK, PLAY AND CELEBRATION are very different things. Giving life over to work is easy. We are, as a society, centered in work. We also, as a people, know how to play. As long as the game is structured we are very good at it, either as participants or as regular, seasonal spectators. What we do not do nearly as well as work and play is to celebrate.

Celebration—unlike work and play—has no product in mind, no trophy to garner. So, why celebrate? What's the use in it?

Celebration is about learning to recognize the gifts of life. Unless and until we can celebrate the gifts in which we are daily immersed but often oblivious—the smell of fresh bread, the understanding of friends, the luxury of silence, the talents of our children, the goodness of our neighbors, the dignity of our lives—life escapes us.

Lack of celebration in life is a sign of the lack of the contemplative dimension of life. Why? Because it is of the essence of the contemplative—the one who has come to see life as God sees life—to see the goodness of creation and to go wild with the joy of it.

Celebration is the gift of loose and lively joy, the gift of a healthy life.

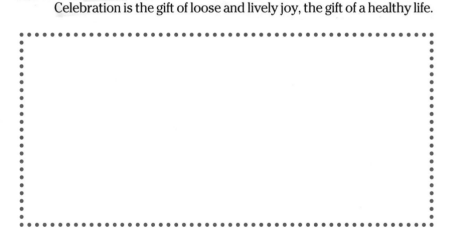

On this mountain our God will provide for all peoples
a feast of rich food and choice wines,
juicy, rich food and pure, choice wines.
Isaiah 25:6

Choosing Life

One day an angel appeared to a seeker hard at work in the field of life and said, "I have been instructed by the gods to inform you that you have three more lives before you gain enlightenment." With that the seeker fell dejectedly into heavy sobbing. "Three more lives, three more lives. Oh no," he cried, "three more lives" and he wailed and rolled in the dust. Then the angel moved on to another seeker bent over by the heat of the day and gave the same message. "I have been sent to tell you," the angel said, "that you will have 10,000 more lives before enlightenment." "Really," the seeker exclaimed. "Ten thousand more lives? Only 10,000 more lives? Only 10,000 more lives and I will be enlightened." And he began to sing and dance joyfully before God. Suddenly a voice came from heaven: "My child, this day you have attained enlightenment."

THE THING ABOUT WINTER is that it snows. The thing about spring is that it rains. The thing about summer is that it's sweltering hot. The thing about autumn is that it's dark and cold. Isn't it wonderful? All of it. Every single different thing that makes us adjust and enjoy and live life differently.

It is an exercise in "yes," this slip-slide from winter to spring to summer to fall. Yes to today; yes to tomorrow; yes to life again. The turn of the seasons is a kaleidoscope of the seasons of life, of the face of God in time, of the very process of what it means to be alive.

In the seasons we see the story of ourselves played out: early on, life without shape; later, life in pursuit of direction; finally, life on the way to its horizon; at the end, life, mellowed, going down into the sea of eternity. Through them all, like warp and woof, lies the essential pattern, the obligation to say "yes."

Yes, yes, yes, life teaches us to say. Yes, yes, yes, we must learn to say back. Otherwise, we will surely die long before we have ever learned to live.

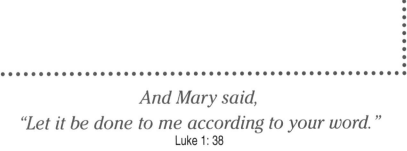

And Mary said,
"Let it be done to me according to your word."
Luke 1: 38

Comfort

*"Once upon a time," an old Hasidic tale teaches us,
the local Jewish congregation was very concerned
about the fact that their rabbi disappeared every single
Sabbath night. Was he chanting with angels? Was he
praying with Elijah? Was he communing directly with
God? So, after months of this, they finally sent someone
to follow him who would report back to them on where
the rabbi was going. Sure enough, the next Sabbath
eve, the rabbi went up a mountain path, over the crest
of the mountain to a cottage on the far side of the cliff.
And there, the sexton could see through the window,
lay an old gentile woman, wasting away sick in bed.
The rabbi swept the floor, chopped the wood, lit the
fire, made a large pot of stew, washed the bedclothes
and then left quickly in order to get back to the syna-
gogue in time for morning services. The sexton, too,
arrived back breathless.*

*"Well," the congregation demanded to know, "did
our rabbi go up to heaven?" The sexton thought for a
minute, "Oh, no, my friends," he said and smiled softly.
"Our rabbi did not go up to heaven. Our rabbi went
much higher than that."*

THERE ARE SOME KINDS OF PAIN that cannot be taken away in life. Loss. Hurt. Rejection. Disability. But those who enter into the pain of another know what it is to talk about the love of a God who does not change the circumstances that form us but walks through them with us every step of the way.

Pain is that dimension of human life that calls us both to give, and sometimes to receive, that awkward, often incomplete but always healing care, to simply sit with those who hurt.

Indeed, comfort is a small and tender thing. All it takes is regular presence, patient listening and genuine concern. Maybe that's why there is so little of it in the world. It demands that we go out of ourselves to the other in ways that advantage us not a wit. In fact, comfort is a very expensive thing.

To go down into pain with another person breaks open the heart of the God who looks among us always for the face most like God's own.

P.S. The real question, come to think about it, is whether or not the congregation kept their old rabbi or got themselves a new one—for the sake of the faith, of course.

Jesus wept.
John 11:33

Commitment

A seeker who has been calling on God for many years finally hears a voice within: "Who is there?" "At last," she thinks and joyfully answers. "God, it is I." But she is met by silence. The door to enlightenment remains closed. Years pass and the woman goes on meditating and calling on God with renewed passion. At last, without warning, she hears the voice again, "Who is there?" This time, without hesitation, she replies, "Only Thou." The door opens and she merges with God.

COMMITMENT IS THAT QUALITY of life that depends more on the ability to wait for something to come to fulfillment—through good days and through bad—than it does on being able to sustain an extreme emotion for it over a long period of time.

When the work ceases to feel good, when praying for peace goes nowhere, when the plans and the hopes worse than fail—they fizzle—that's when the commitment really starts. When enthusiasm wanes, and romantic love dies, and moral apathy—a debilitating loss of purpose and energy—sets in, that is the point at which we are asked to turn an adventure into a commitment.

Commitment is that quality of human nature that tells us not to count days or months or years, conversations or efforts or rejections, but simply to go on going on until "all things are in the fullness of time," until everything is ready, until all hearts are in waiting for the Word of God in this situation to be fulfilled.

When we feel most discouraged, most fatigued, most alone is precisely the time we must not quit.

My soul waits for you; I count on your word.
Psalm 130:5

Death

"What would you say to a close friend who is about to die?" Jiddu Krishnamurti asked a small group of listeners. The answers dealt with assurances, words about beginnings and endings, and various gestures of compassion. Krishnamurti stopped them short. "There is only one thing you can say to give the deepest comfort," he said. "Tell them that in his death a part of you dies and goes with him. Wherever he goes, you go also; he will not be alone."

DEATH SEEMS SO CRUEL, so purposeless at times. But it's not. Death is what alerts the rest of us to life—just when we have grown tired of it ourselves, perhaps, or worse yet, simply unaware of it all.

Death is the call to look again at life—this time with a wiser eye. Life, for the likes of us, is not a series of struggles and irritations. That, it seems, is reserved for refugees and farm families on hard soil and peasant types on mountaintops and in barrios. Our life, on the other hand, is a panoply of opportunities. It does not depend on "luck." It depends on what we do with it, how we approach it, what we make of what we have, how we distinguish between wants and needs—and, most of all, how much of ourselves we put into making it better, not only for ourselves, but for those who lack the resources even to begin to make it better for themselves.

Death, the awareness of its coming, is what calls us to a life beyond apathy, beyond indifference, beyond concern. Death reminds us to live.

Death gives us all the gift of time. Our own time and the time of those around us. It calls us to stop and look at the sunflowers next time, to care for the trees always, to embrace the planet forever, to pay attention to our friends.

Teach us the shortness of life
that we may gain wisdom of heart.
Psalm 90:12

Discipleship

Once there was a student who was with a teacher for many years. And, when the teacher felt he was going to die, he wanted to make even his death a lesson. That night, the teacher took a torch, called his student, and set off with him through the forest. Soon they reached the middle of the woods where the teacher extinguished the torch, without explanation. "What is the matter?" asked the student. "The torch has gone out," the teacher answered and walked on. "But," shouted the student, his voice plucking his fear, "will you leave me here in the dark?" "No! I will not leave you in the dark," returned his teacher's voice from the surrounding blackness. "I will leave you searching for the light."

DISCIPLESHIP IS WATCHING and learning from the experience and wisdom of another in order to become the kind of spiritual adult ourselves that we recognize them to be. Clearly, the purpose of the spiritual master is to enable us to grow to our own full stature. It is not meant to make us childish; it is meant to lead us to maturity.

The important thing is to beware the guru, the mentor, the

leader who doesn't bring you to respect and follow your own authority. Too many mentors confuse spiritual leadership with authoritarianism and control. Too many people use their position, their authority to keep another person in emotional bondage in order to satisfy their own egos.

Beware the leader, any leader, any system, who takes away from you either your conscience or your individual call. When you discover that you have given up your own insights, your own intuitions, your own wisdom to the control of another, you have given up discipleship for mental slavery. That's why the Zen masters teach, "If you meet the Buddha on the road, kill him."

I am the light of the world,
whoever follows me will never walk in darkness
but will have the light of life.
John 8:12

Enlightenment

*"Master, I come to you seeking enlightenment," the
priest said to the Holy One. "Well, then," the master
said, "for the first exercise of your retreat, go into the
courtyard, tilt back your head, stretch out your arms and
wait until I come for you." Just as the priest arranged
himself in the garden the rain came. And it rained.
And it rained. And it rained. Finally, the old master
came back. "Well, priest," he said, "have you been
enlightened today?" "Are you serious," the priest said in
disgust. "I've been standing here with my head up in the
rain for an hour. I'm soaking wet and I feel like a fool!"
And the master said, "Well, priest, for the first day of a
retreat that sounds like great enlightenment to me."*

THE ONE MAJOR FUNCTION of darkness in this world, whatever kind of
darkness it may be, is always, in the final analysis, enlightenment.
What we learn when we cannot see our way through a hard place in
life are insights that we have failed to discern in better situations.

We hear a great deal about loss in life, for instance, but we never really come to know intangible presence until someone we really love dies. We read one article after another on simplicity of life but we never really come to realize how little it takes to be happy until we lose something of great significance.

Philosophers and theologians debate eternally what every human being, one way or another, comes to know without doubt: Life is a process of watching the material dimensions of the human condition slip away while the spirit grows stronger, greater, richer all the way to eternity. All the while our bodies wane, the spirit is waxing. It is the paradox of life. That's why no one is ever ready to die. The older we get the more we are just beginning to understand life and to really live it well. That process is called enlightenment.

Send your light and your truth; let these be my guide.
Lead me to your holy mountain,
to the place where you dwell.
Psalm 43:3

Feeding the Hungry

*Once on the Great Sabbath the rabbi of Roptchitz
came home from the house of prayer with weary steps.
"What made you so tired?" asked his wife. "It was the
sermon," the rabbi replied. "I had to speak of the poor
and their many needs for the coming Passover. Unleavened
bread and wine and everything else is terribly
high this year." "And what did you accomplish with
your sermon?" his wife asked. "Half of what is needed,"
he answered. "You see, the poor are now ready to take.
As for the other half, whether the rich are ready to
give—I don't know about that yet."*

THIS WEEK A MAN WALKED into our soup kitchen, gave an envelope
to one of the sisters and said, "This envelope comes with two
conditions: the first is that you tell no one where you got it, and
the second is that you give it to the poor." Inside the envelope
there were 50 twenty-dollar bills.

The very thought of it nourishes our souls as much as it
nourished the bodies and souls of those to whom it was given.
Indeed, people who live close to the edge of survival, barely

clinging to family and dignity and hope, struggle against dryness of soul, starvation of the heart, sourness of the spirit. They sit in the doorways of our cities and remind us all of our needs, spiritual if not physical.

The point is clear: there is something more important than "rugged individualism" that threatens to destroy us all. It is our lack of care for one another. The gospel imperative to feed the hungry, to give drink to the thirsty is not about giving things away at all. It's about all of us—those who need and those who give—finally getting to be more human together.

For where your treasure is,
there will your heart be also.
Luke 12:34

Food and Celebration

In Vietnam there is a traditional folk image of the difference between heaven and hell. In hell, people have chopsticks a yard long so that they cannot reach their mouths. In heaven, the chopsticks are the same length—but the people feed one another.

ONE DAY, in one of those great life inventory games that has become so popular in an age of humanistic psychology and personal development exercises, I was part of a seminar that asked us to list ten of your warmest memories. It was easy. I wrote them all down quickly. And they all involved food: summer picnics on the peninsula, our family's Irish wakes, dad's cinnamon toast, packing sandwiches for our fishing trips, smelling my mother's oyster stew....

It didn't take long before I realized that it wasn't the food that I remembered. It was the occasion and all it meant, year after year after year. All those things had marked my way through life. They were the things I waited for. They were the moments that made life special and family real and life fun. The food was simply the sign that all those things were still safe, still functioning, still the stuff of life.

The oyster stew and the watermelon, the fresh bread for sandwiches and the bottle of wine to go with them, the smell of Christmas ham and Thanksgiving turkey, the holidays and birthdays and picnics and family specialties all serve to remind us still of the glory of God, the bounty of God, the blessedness of life, the proof that life, in the end, is always good.

The kingdom of heaven may be compared to a king who gave a feast for his son's wedding.
Matthew 22:2

Freedom

The young monk asked the master: "How can I ever get emancipated?" The master answered, "Who has ever put you in bondage?"

VIKTOR FRANKL, Jewish psychiatrist and survivor of the Nazi prison camps, wrote extensively after World War II about the effect of the camps on the psyches and souls of the inmates as well as on their bodies. Most importantly, his intense exploration of the subjects in his now classic work, *Man's Search for Meaning*, has special meaning for anyone—everyone—who find themselves trapped in a meaningless, destructive or oppressive situation.

In the midst of the fanaticism of Nazi anti-Semitism—its burning crematoria and medical experiments, its ruthless death marches and starvation diets—Frankl discovered that the final effect of such brutality, physical or psychological, lay not with the oppressors at all but with the oppressed themselves.

In the end, Frankl proposed, no one can destroy us unless we give them the power over us that enables them to do it. Unless we ourselves give in to the message of the oppressor, the oppressor may, of course, be able to constrain us or control us or even kill us. But they cannot take our sense of self, our sense of worth, our sense of purpose, our sense of right. They cannot even take away our sense of freedom.

We are all imprisoned somewhere, by something. But the attitude we choose for ourselves will determine whether the present "prison" we're in has the power to destroy us or not.

She cried out, being in labor and about to give birth…. And the dragon stood before the woman who was about to give birth, so that when she gave birth he might devour the child. And she gave birth…and her child was caught up in God.

Revelation 12:2-5

God's Presence

*"How does one seek union with God?" the seeker
asked. "The harder you seek, the more distance you
create between God and you," the elder answered.
"So what does one do about the distance?" the seeker
persisted. "Understand that it isn't there," the elder
answered. "Does that mean that God and I are one?"
the seeker continued. "Not one, not two," the elder
answered. "But how is that possible?" the seeker cried,
dismayed. "The sun and its light, the ocean and the
wave, the singer and the song—not one, not two," the
elder answered.*

HOW DO I KNOW that God is present? The question has an urgency
to it. It carries within itself the foundations of morality, the purpose
of life. The elder in the story makes the point: God and I are not
the same thing but God is the essence of everything that is. God,
in other words, is everywhere, as truly in those things where we
are sure that God is missing as in those things that we are sure are
infallible signs of the presence of God.

The presence of God does not depend on an act of God's will; it depends simply on our own realization that where I am, God is. The challenge is to come to the point that where God is, I am. Wherever. Whenever. It is not a case of God being present to me. It is a case of my being present to God. The sure sign that we are living in the presence of God is the way we see and respond to the rest of the world. Those who have cultivated the presence of God, see the world as God sees the world. And they respond accordingly.

For it was you who formed me
in my inmost being;
you knit me together in my mother's womb.
Psalm 139:13

Goodness

She has been so wicked that in all her life she had done only one good deed—given an onion to a beggar. So she went to hell. As she lay in torment she saw the onion, lowered down from heaven by an angel. She caught hold of it. The angel began to pull it up. The other damned saw what was happening and caught hold on it, too. She was indignant and cried, "Let go—it's my onion," and as soon as she said, "my onion," the stalk broke and she fell back into the flames.

SHAKESPEARE, in the classic *Hamlet* says about everything we need to know about the tension between what is goodness and what is really goodness. In Act 1, scene V Hamlet says, "That one may smile, and smile, and be a villain."

The insight, at first look, seems obvious but the trick is for us to avoid the pitfall that comes with virtue gone bad. When the church protects pedophile priests in order to save the church rather than the children, the instinct may be understandable but it is not right. When Jesuit Dan Berrigan spent years in jail for protesting nuclear weapons in order to call the attention of the country to the devastating effects of nuclearism on children everywhere, here as well as in war zones, goodness, generosity, and love glowed into a flame seen around the world.

Down deep, we always know the difference between the good and the really good. Down deep we can always smell spoiled virtue even when we can't see it. In a society thick with corporate wealth and poor on social services, we can see the distance between goodness and greatness, between compassion that is real and the kind of humanity that is rare.

You are the light of the world....
Let your light shine in the sight of all,
so that, seeing your good works,
others may praise God.
Matthew 5: 14, 16

Guilt

Once a brother committed a sin in Scetis and the elders assembled and sent for Abba Moses. He, however, did not want to go. Then the priest sent a message to him, saying: "Come, everyone is waiting for you." So Abba Moses got up to go. And he took a worn-out basket with holes, filled it with sand, and carried it along.

The people who came to meet him said, "What is this, Father?" Then the old man said, "My sins are running out behind me, yet I do not see them. And today I have come to judge the sins of someone else." When they heard this, they said nothing to the brother, and pardoned him.

GUILT IS A VERY FUNNY THING. In fact, I remember laughing very hard one day at a very simple joke: "I hear you're not working for that psychiatrist anymore. I thought you liked the job," the friend said. "I did," she answered. "Then why did you quit?" the friend insisted. "Well, you see," she said, "when I was late, he said I was passive-aggressive. When I was early, he said I was obsessive-compulsive. And when I was on time, he said I was anal-retentive. That's more guilt than any one person should bear in any one lifetime, so I quit."

The joke helps us to see how guilt, used to control a person, can be a weapon of terrible spiritual as well as psychological destruction. It begins in diminishment and ends in self-hatred. That kind of guilt should be fled like the plague.

On the other hand, guilt—the awareness that we want to be more than we are—can be the call to a far better self. But the real purpose of guilt is to enable us to remember that we have no right to accuse the other. The goal of life is not being sinless. It is being good that life is all about.

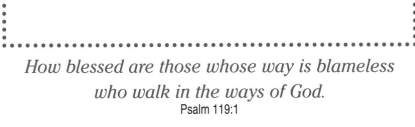

How blessed are those whose way is blameless
who walk in the ways of God.
Psalm 119:1

On Happiness

"What good work shall I do to be acceptable to God?"
the disciple asked the rabbi.

"How should I know?" the rabbi answered. "Abraham practiced hospitality and God was with him. Elias loved to pray and God was with him. David ruled a kingdom and God was with him, too. Judith led the people and God was by her side."

"Well, then," the disciple said, "is there some way I can find my own allotted work?"

"Yes," said the rabbi. "Search for the deepest inclination of your heart and follow it."

ONE THING FOR SURE: the nature of happiness is one of the great universal riddles of all time. The answers vary and often collide but it is the riddle itself that is important. Not to ask myself, Am I happy? is to fail to ask what may be the greatest spiritual development question of all time. The answer to What is happiness? may itself be a question: Are you doing what you like to do and are you doing it in such a way that it makes life better for others? Aristotle called happiness "the activity of soul in conformity with excellence." To be the best human being we can be, in other words, whatever it is that we do: to be capable workers, to be good parents, to be kind neighbors. And then Aristotle gave the most important insight of all. He said, "But we must add 'In a complete life,' for one swallow does not make a summer." It all takes time. Happiness is something we develop, not something we get.

Happy are the people with such blessings.
Psalm 144:15

Heart of the Matter

A holy one said to a merchant, "As the fish perishes on dry land, so you perish when you get entangled in the world. The fish must return to the water and you must return to the spiritual." The merchant was aghast. "Are you saying that I must give up my business and go into a monastery?" And the holy one said, "Oh, no, no, never. I am saying, hold on to your business but go into your heart."

IT IS NOT SO MUCH what we do but the spirit with which we do it that counts. The only thing worth spending my life on is something that makes life richer, warmer, fuller, happier where I am. All the great projects in the world will not forgive my selfishness, my arrogance, my harshness with others. We are each given only one life. The spirit we bring to it, the heart we put into it is the measure of its value, whatever else we do with it to make a living. It isn't difficult to be good at what we do. What is difficult is to be great about the way we do it.

The purpose of life is one thing. It has to do with choosing to pursue the lofty as opposed to the ignoble. The purpose of my life is entirely another. That has to do with choosing to spend myself in ways that bring holiness to the mundane. The problem is that only I can do it. How I am, the environment around me will be: full of arsenic or full of the warmth of the Spirit.

I have come to set fire to the earth,
and I wish it were already blazing.
Luke 12:49

Honoring the Other

"What is the deepest meaning of Buddhism, Master?"
the disciple asked. And the master turned to the student
and bowed.

I HAD BEEN IN MANY international settings many times in my life before this one. This time was very different. This time we were all there—Christians, Jews, Muslims, Buddhists, Hindus and every variety of each—to join together as women, as professional religious figures to bring women into peacemaking arenas of the world in order to demonstrate the peace we sought in the religions we followed.

The schedule called for a "Day of Prayer." At first, it seemed like it was going to be a long day of foreign recitations. But then, little by little, women began to join in. The singing got stronger; the chanting got fuller; the room got quieter, deeper, calmer. We weren't strangers anymore. We had honored a common God. God had taken all of us beyond our one tongue to the God of many tongues. Or God had become bigger—and we, as well. The one God had brought us all into Oneness.

I understood something that day in a way I never had before: Beware the religion that turns you against another one. It's unlikely that it's really religion at all.

Mary brought in a pound of very costly ointment, pure nard, and with it anointed the feet of Jesus, wiping them with her hair; the house was full of the scent of the ointment.
John 12: 3

Hospitality

There was a monastery that was renowned for its hospitality, a welcoming place for many weary travelers in need of rest. One day while the abbot was deep in prayer an angel appeared, surrounded by golden light. The abbot gazed in rapt contemplation and was filled with a peace beyond measure. Suddenly a series of heavy knocks resounded on the front door. "It is some weary traveler come to find shelter," the abbot said to himself. "What should I do? If I go and answer the door, the angel might disappear. If I stay, who will care for the traveler?"

Reluctantly the abbot rose, looked resignedly at the angel, and left the room in order to attend to the needs of the dust-stained traveler.

When he returned to his cell, the angel, to the abbot's great surprise, was still there. The angel said to him, "Had you not gone to help the needy traveler, I myself would have been compelled to leave."

IT DOESN'T TAKE A LOT of thinking to understand why qualities like honesty, self-control, devotion and love are components of the spiritual life. But hospitality—the fine art of being nice to people? Why—of all things—hospitality? The question captures the imagination of the soul.

Why is it that one of the oldest spiritual documents in Western civilization, the *Rule of Benedict*, says hardly a word about asceticism but speaks over and over again about hospitality and the reception of guests?

The answer, I think, is that hospitality is basic. It's hospitality that teaches us honesty and self-control, devotion and love, openness and trust. The way of hospitality is more difficult—and more meaningful—than any asceticism we could devise for ourselves.

Desert monastics, spiritual seekers who went into the backwaters of Egypt and the Middle East to live a life of solitude and prayer, broke every rule they lived by on behalf of hospitality because to wander through a desert without water and without help is, in the final analysis, to condemn the traveler to death. Hospitality is the fine art of having an open soul and a listening mind in a world where, alone, we would all die from starvation of the soul.

Guardian of the orphan, defender of the widowed,
such is God who gives the lonely a home.
Psalm 68:5-6

Humility

The disciple said to the teacher, "I want to make a good impression on people. What should I strive for?" And the teacher answered, "If I had been asked in the first years of my spiritual quest what I wanted people to say in appreciation of me, I would have answered, "Let them say he is a holy man." Years later I would have answered, "Let them say he is a loving man." And now I would like people to say of me, "He is a free man."

THE FIRST TIME I SAW IT was in the eyes of an old monk. He had been revered as a teacher. But, most of all, he was recognized for the depth of his reflections, the scope of his vision. He had even written a book that had been translated into six languages. Who was this man, I wondered?

Then one night at a conference, I found myself sitting next to him at the dinner table. "Tell me about your book," I said. He smiled a teasing little smile. "What would you like to know about it?" he came back. "Well," I stumbled on, "I hear it's been translated into six languages." "Oh yes," he said. "It got the Theological Booksellers

Award—and sold 280 copies." Then he threw back his head and laughed. Out loud and long. He couldn't have cared less. He simply did what he did because he thought it should be done.

I will hear that laugh as long as I live. It was so freeing.

That is the kind of freedom—freedom from the self, freedom for the gospel—that changes things. It is a gift of no small value, a grace of no small proportion. Unfortunately, it is also too little prized—and so, both we and the world stay in chains.

One Sabbath day he was teaching in one of the synagogues, and a woman was there who for eighteen years had been possessed by a spirit that left her enfeebled; she was bent double and quite unable to stand upright. When Jesus saw her he called her over and said, "Woman, you are rid of your infirmity" and he laid his hands on her. And at once she straightened up, and she glorified God.

Luke 13:10-13

Laughter

*The disciples came to the Master and said, "Teach us
how to pray." This is how she taught them...Two men
were walking through a field when they saw an angry
bull in hot pursuit. It soon became evident to them that
they were not going to make it, so one man shouted
to the other, "We've had it! Nothing can save us. Say
a prayer. Quick!" The other shouted back, "I haven't
prayed since I was a child." "Never mind," the first man
shouted, "the bull is catching up with us. Any prayer will
do." "Well," the second man yelled, "I do remember one
prayer that my father used to say before meals: For what
we are about to receive, God, make us truly grateful."*

MY GOD IS A GOD WHO LAUGHS. And why not?

Laughter gives us the freedom of the Jesus who foolishly
questioned the authority of the state and smilingly stretched the
imagination of the church. "The poor shall inherit the Kingdom,"
he laughed. "The kingdom of heaven is like a woman," he smiled.
"God is daddy," he chuckled. He danced from town to town, healing,
making people smile with new hope, bringing invitations to people
in trees and light-footedness to lepers. He fished where there were
no fish. He invited guests to eat with him when he had no food. He
taught babies and poked fun at Pharisees and told winsome little

stories, spiritual jokes about women who would not let pretentious judges alone.

Day after day he smiled his way from one theological absolute to another and left the world with enough to smile about till the end of time.

Once we learn to laugh and play, we will have come closer to understanding our laughing, playing God. The God of the ridiculous promises is a God who laughs, a God to be laughed at and laughed with, until that moment when all pain washes away and only the laughter of God is left to be heard in the heavens.

When God brought Israel back to Zion,
it seemed like a dream.
Then our mouths were filled with laughter;
on our lips there were songs of joy.
Psalm 126:1-2

Love

Ananda, the beloved disciple of the Buddha, once asked his teacher about the place of friendship in the spiritual journey. "Master, is friendship half of the spiritual life?" he asked. And the teacher responded, "Nay, Ananda, friendship is the whole of the spiritual life."

LOVE IS SOMETHING LEARNED only by the long, hard labor of life. It is sometimes over before we've ever known we ever had it. We sometimes destroy it before we appreciate it. We often take it for granted. Every love, whatever happens to it in the long run, teaches us more about ourselves, our needs, our limitations, and our self-centeredness than anything else we can ever experience. As Aldous Huxley wrote: "There isn't any formula or method. You learn by loving."

But sometimes, if we're lucky, we live long enough to grow into it in such a way that because of it we come to recognize the value of life. As the years go by, we come to love flowers and cats and small infants and old ladies and the one person in life who knows how hot we like our coffee. We learn enough about love to allow things to slip away and ourselves to melt into the God whose love made all of it possible. Sometimes we even find a love deep enough, gentle enough, tender enough to detach us from the foam and frills of life, all of which hold us captive to things that cannot satisfy. Sometimes we live long enough to see the face of God in another. Then, in that case, we have loved.

Love never ends.
1 Cor. 13:8

Mercy

"Who is closer to God," the seeker asked, "the saint or the sinner?" "Why the sinner, of course," the elder said. "But how can that be?" the seeker asked. "Because," the elder said, "every time a person sins they break the cord that binds them to God. But every time God forgives them, the cord is knotted again. And so, thanks to the mercy of God, the cord gets shorter and the sinner closer to God."

THIS SOCIETY is locked in mortal combat between mercy and justice. On which side must we err, if err we must? Which side do we want for ourselves when we cut corners, bend the rules, break the codes, succumb to needs not being met in other places and ways? Which side is right?

What we never seem to consider, however, is that mercy and justice may be the same thing. What is justice, after all, but the ability to mete out what is deserved? That's why justice and mercy are one. We are made of dust, not gold, remember? And dust is worthy of little but mercy. Now that is great luck.

We forget that it can be merciful to restrain a person from harming either themselves or others. We fail to remember that it can be the highest form of justice to practice mercy. Until, that is, one day we need them both ourselves. Until we examine our own lives and the lives of those we love and find them bathed in mercy where many would have said that justice was required. Then, we understand God a little better. Then we understand both mercy and justice in a different way.

Mercy and faithfulness meet;
justice and peace embrace.
Psalm 85:10

Mysticism

Abba Lot went to see Abba Joseph and said, "Abba, as much as I am able, I practice a small rule, all the little fasts, some prayer and meditation, and, as much as possible I keep my thoughts clean. What else should I do?

The old man stood up and stretched out his hands towards heaven, and his fingers became like the torches of flame. And he said, "Why not be turned into fire?"

THE DIFFERENCE BETWEEN religion and spirituality is the difference between orthodoxy and mysticism. The orthodox are those who keep the rules and guard the creeds of all the denominations of the world. They know a heretic when they see one.

The mystics of every religion are those who are looking for more than the security that the rules give in order to absorb the spirit to which the rules are meant to refer. They go beyond theology to immerse themselves in the reality which the rules are designed to prepare us to see and the theology is meant to describe. They go beyond the ritual to the reality to which it points. They melt into God. They embrace the whole world. They become love and compassion.

Mystics go beyond the norms of every religion to the God every religion is established to revere. Then, denominational boundaries disappear, differences dissolve, theological distinctions become meaningless and we find ourselves welded to the presence of God here and now. In everything. Everywhere. At all times.

...may you know the breadth and length and height and depth of the love of Christ that is beyond all knowledge... so you may attain to fullness of being, the fullness of God.
Ephesians 3-18-19

Nature

A philosopher asked Saint Antony: "How can you be enthusiastic when the comfort of books has been taken away from you?" He replied: "My book, O Philosopher, is the nature of created things, and whenever I want to read the word of God, it is usually right in front of me."

THE MEETING PLACE for our session in Tokyo, they told me, was through the double doors to the left of the elevator. I was not surprised to find the elevator padded with brass-studded leather. The fact that the carpet in the corridor was thick and soft seemed usual enough. The real surprise, however, was the fact that beyond the heavy oak doors, the meeting room was not the average conference room of large round tables and fold-up metal chairs

Instead, there was nothing in this maroon and gold draped room but one needle-nosed red celadon vase that held one fresh yellow rose. One rose in the vase on a glass table in the middle of a room draped in red and gold velvet. Nothing but pure mindfulness, pure reverence, pure life. This room, you had to think, had been built for this one vase and this single rose.

The stark attention, the sentinel awareness, the utterly concentrated focus on one rose steeped the room in the consciousness of beauty.

Focusing on one thing in nature every day—one rose in a beautiful vase, one old tree gnarled but indomitable, one rugged mountain range undiminished by time, or whatever it is that calls us to reverence the mystery that is life—is meditation enough to make life precious whatever its stressors.

Let everything that has breath praise our God.
Psalm 150:6

Open-mindedness

A seeker went to visit a Holy One hoping for enlighten-
ment. The Holy One invited the seeker into her cell
and offered her a drink. "Yes, a drink would be fine,"
said the seeker. The Holy One poured until the seek-
er's glass was full and then kept pouring. The seeker
watched until she could take it no longer. "It is over-
full," the seeker said. "No more will go into it." "Like
the glass," the Holy One said, "you are full of your own
truths, ideas and opinions. You cannot be enlightened
until you first empty your glass."

ALVIN TOFFLER WROTE ONCE, "The poor of the future will not be those
who cannot read and write but those who cannot learn, unlearn
and relearn." It is openness to living into a future without canned
answers that will really count.

More important, perhaps, than openness of the citizens
of such a culture to new ideas, may well be the openness of the
institutions of such a culture to their continuing development.

Close-mindedness is a terrible thing. It stops thought. It

blocks thought. It freezes thought. It demands obedience to ignorance. It preaches the past in the name of sanctity. It insults thinking people by refusing to allow them to think. It assumes that only some of us have the right to think at all.

Governments do it; churches do it; schools do it; corporations do it; parents do it; ideologues of all stripes and motives do it.

Perhaps never in the history of the world have we needed to take so seriously again the corporal work of mercy to "instruct the ignorant." But this time, it may be more important that the institutions of society take instruction more earnestly than the people we are all so arrogantly inclined to treat as ignorant.

...and the truth will set you free.
John 8:32

Openness

Once upon a time a man, whose ax was missing, sus-pected his neighbor's son. The boy walked like a thief and spoke like a thief. But the man found his ax while digging in the valley, and the next time he saw his neighbor's son, the boy walked, looked and spoke like any other child.

—Lao Tzu

THE OLD LADY LIMPED slowly up a mobile platform and stood there waiting while the men rolled it along in front of the dais to the speaker's stand. Then, holding onto the podium as she moved, she struggled into place behind the microphone. I groaned inwardly. "Oh, no," I thought, not another "When I was young" speech. After all, what else could an old lady do in a gathering like this.

When she began to speak, she commanded every inch of the room. She held every eye, controlled every thought, stilled every movement in the hall. I had never heard such applause when she finished. I had never experienced such respect for a living person. A woman. An old woman.

And I did learn that night. Plenty. I learned not to decide

whether or not I like things before I try them. The government insists that all packages be labeled so we have some kind of precise awareness of what they contain. Too bad we don't do the same thing with people. As in: tattoos are not harmful to your health, dreadlocks are not harmful to your health, color is not dangerous to your social life, and age is not a disease that affects either intelligence or effectiveness. It could save us a lot of time and a lot of human mistakes. In the meantime, it seems, only open-heartedness can possibly save us from ourselves.

The Samaritan woman said to Jesus,
"What? You are a Jew and you ask me,
a Samaritan, for a drink?""""
Jews do not associate with Samaritans.
John 4:9

Passion

A seeker went to the monastery to gain enlightenment. He prayed and prayed, but nothing happened. When it came time to leave, the disappointed visitor went to the master and asked, "Why has my stay here yielded no fruit?" "Could it be because you lacked the courage to shake the tree?" said the master benignly.

PASSION IS THE HEARTBEAT of life. We all know passionate people. Sometimes we might even look at them and shake our heads. But in that case, we need to be careful. They are in our lives to model for us exactly what we may need to know about the fine art of living.

Passionate people change the world. They bring it color and skill, joy and focus, interest and excitement. They show us how to live with intensity and care.

We have been taught to fear passion, however. What a pity. What we have not been well taught, perhaps, is that a life without passion is a dull life indeed. Maybe even a very limited one. Certainly a barren one. Without passion, life turns routine. Blah sets in.

What we do with our passions, how we control them, how we nurture them, how we direct them, determines what will become of us the rest of our lives. More than that, perhaps, it determines who we are.

Passion, you see, is one of the hallmarks of being human. And it is everywhere. The only question is whether or not there is really enough of it.

*I know all about
how you are neither cold nor hot.
I wish you were one or the other,
but since you are neither, only lukewarm,
I will spit you out of my mouth.*
Revelation 3:15-16

Paths of Life

The Westerner, excited to be on a safari for the first time, force-marched his native guides through the jungle on a wild search for game, any game at all. The party made good speed the first two days but on the third morning, when it was time to start, the hunter found all the guides sitting on their haunches looking very solemn and making no preparations to leave. "What are they doing?" the man asked. "Why aren't we moving on?" "They are waiting," the chief guide explained. "They cannot move farther until their souls catch up with their bodies."

I REMEMBER ALL MY LIFE being asked what I had decided to do with my years on this earth.

The question had me fooled. I always thought you were supposed to have an answer. And the funny thing is that no answer I came up with was ever final, was ever really "right."

I studied English and wound up a history teacher. I went to graduate school and, just before I finished the degree, found myself out of teaching completely and about to be an administrator.

Finally, I began to understand: it's really not so much what you choose to do in life that counts. It won't last anyway. No, in the end, it's not necessarily what you decide; it's how you handle it when what you decide doesn't happen the way you plan it. It's about how you slip and slide from one place to the next, how you adjust. It's how you grow, which in the end, makes all the difference.

It's not the path; it's the learning, the life along the way that makes the journey. Or as Carlos Castaneda puts it, "Does this path have a heart?" Does it have meaning, seek meaning? Answer: Only if we make it so.

You will show me the path of life
and guide me to joy forever.
Psalm 16:11

Praying the Scriptures

A rabbi always told his people that if they studied the Torah, it would put scripture on their hearts. One of them asked, "Why 'on' our hearts, and not 'in' them?" The rabbi answered, "Only God can put scripture inside. But reading sacred text can put in on your hearts, and then when the heart breaks, the holy words will fall inside."

SO MANY THINGS break a heart open in life. Sometimes it's beauty, often it's pain, always it's love. Sometimes it is the sheer weariness of getting up day after day after day to the life that never happens.

Then what happens to us?

The rabbi says that it all depends on what we have been putting on our hearts all these years.

Only if we have stayed close to the scriptures, to the story of God's presence in life, can we bear any burden, survive any loss, absorb however much beauty without dying from the breathless glory of it, and give ourselves to the other side of love—the side that gives as well as takes.

It is the scriptures on our heart that remind us of "the lilies of the field," the despair of the woman who "had not stood up straight for 30 years," the emptiness of the day before the Resurrection, the exhilaration of those who first say, "I have seen the Christ."

Praying the scriptures, regular and unceasing, is what prepares us for life in all its dimensions.

And Jesus said to them,
"Today this scripture is fulfilled in your hearing."
Luke 4:21

Purpose of Life

Rabbi Akiba was in the midst of a long journey and stopped at a town to lodge along the way. None of the townspeople, however, would give him a room. So Akiba took his only three possessions—a lamp, a rooster and a donkey—to a field outside of town and settled down for the night. While he slept, the wind blew out his lamp, a cat devoured his rooster and a lion ate his donkey. Now, he had no light for the night, no food for the journey and no way to complete the trip. Undeterred, Akiba said, "Whatever the Merciful One does, it is done for the best," and went back to sleep.

That very night a band of thieves raided the town and carried off half the population to sell to the caravans. "I am sad for them," he said, "but their turning me away from the town simply proves even further that whatever the Merciful One does, it is done for the best. And, had the light been burning, and the rooster crowing and the donkey braying, I could also have been abducted as well."

THERE IS A DARK PERIOD of life from which it seems there is no liberation. If, all of a sudden, we discover that life has lost its sense of purpose for us, the dark closes in, smothers our hearts, blinds our steps, leaves us swimming in a sea of uselessness. Getting up in the morning takes all the energy we have. Going to work becomes a grind. Caring for what we cared about before this comes to full stop. Why? we ask. Why anything? Why everything? The ancients were well acquainted with the problem. They called it acedia, listlessness, a poisoning of the will. And they had two answers for it. The first is reflected in the Zen saying: "O marvel of marvels," the enlightened one says, "I chop wood; I draw water from the well." It is, in other words, in the daily, the ordinary, the regular, the necessary that the soul grows and the heart expands. It is by doing what we must that we come to enlightenment in life, seeing it for what it is and giving ourselves to make it better. And the second answer is found in the story of Rabbi Akiba. Life is about coming to an awareness of the ordinary and learning to trust the loving presence of God in what we too often regard as burdens. Then, we will indeed have life and have it more abundantly.

*I have come that you may have life
and have it more abundantly.*
John 10:10

Relationships

An old monk lived in a small hut in a country infested with robbers. He called it the Home of Peace. One night a robber broke into the hut in search of money. With his dagger drawn, the thief crept toward the monk. The monk was sitting very still, wrapped in deep meditation. Just as the robber got ready to plunge the knife, the old monk opened his eyes. There was absolutely no fear in them. Instead, he looked at the robber with great compassion and tenderness. The robber hesitated, then dropped his dagger and fell to his knees. The old monk rose and put his arms around the would-be murderer saying, "The ways to realize God are not many, but only one—love."

VALENTINE'S DAY was supposed to be a very happy time in grade school. But, as often as not, it left in its wake a good many sorrowing children. The problem was that some kids didn't give cards to everyone. And however many valentines we did or did not get, we learned young that not having a real friend made life painful. Having a real friend made life special.

The older we got, the more clearly we discovered how right we were. It is the relationships we make as we go which, in the end, give life the only real lasting happiness it will ever have.

One thing we know for sure: Not all relationships last—for one reason or the other—but all relationships are lasting. Even the ones that have hurt us the most leave a lasting impression on our lives. Sometimes especially the ones that have hurt us the most. But the loves that shape us come in many forms: Maybe it will be someone who mentored us as we grew. Maybe it will be a love that ended. Maybe it will be a marriage that lasts beyond its years. Maybe it will be a love that dies too soon. Maybe it will be the companion who goes with us down into every valley, up every mountain of our lives.

All we know as we get older is that it's not the number of valentines we get that count. It's the ones that last that make all the difference in the end.

But Ruth said, "Do not urge me to leave you
and turn back from your company
for wherever you go, I will go,
wherever you live, I will live.
Your people shall be my people, and your God, my God.
Ruth 1:16

Sabbath

Once upon a time, two thieves were undergoing trial by ordeal. It they could walk a wire over the gorge, they would be considered innocent and spared. If, on the other hand, they did not cross the gorge success-fully, the belief was that they had been "executed" by the gods for their guilt. On this particular day, the first thief reached the other side. The second thief, terri-fied, called to him across the chasm, "How did you do it?" And the first thief shouted back, "I don't know. All I know is that when I felt myself tottering to one side, I leaned to the other."

THE FIRST REASON for the Sabbath, the rabbis teach, is to equalize the rich and poor. Safe from the threat of labor on the Sabbath, the poor lived for at least one day a week with the same kind of freedom that the rich enjoyed. The Sabbath is God's gift to the dignity of humankind. It forces us to concentrate on who we are rather than on what we do.

The second reason for the Sabbath, the rabbis say, is to lead us to evaluate our work. As God did on the seventh day, we are also asked to determine whether or not what we are doing in life is really "good." Good for ourselves, good for the people around us, good for the development of the world.

The third reason for the Sabbath, the Hebrew tradition teaches us, is very unlike the American compulsion to turn Sunday into more of the same—only louder, faster and longer. Sabbath is to lead us to reflect on life itself—where we've been, where we're going and why. Sabbath time takes quiet and serious thought and a search for meaning.

Let's see now: If God built rest into the human cycle for one day out of every seven, or 52 days a year, or 3,640 days in the average lifespan of 70 years, that's about ten years out of every lifetime, I'm confused. Tell me again, why are you tired?

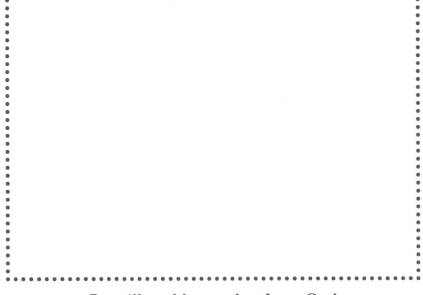

Be still and know that I am God.
Psalm 46:10

Self Acceptance

A man who took great pride in his lawn found himself with a large crop of dandelions. He tried every method he knew to get rid of them. Still they plagued him.

Finally he wrote the Department of Agriculture. He enumerated all the things he had tried and closed his letter with the question: "What shall I do now?"

In due course the reply came, "We suggest you learn to love them."

SELF-KNOWLEDGE GIVES US perspective and self-esteem gives us confidence but it's self-acceptance that gives us peace of heart. It implies, of course, that I know myself and value myself. Yet, unless I can simply start by accepting myself, it is possible that neither of the other two dimensions can ever come to life in me. Clearly, even if I know who I am, even if I admit the truth about myself, if I don't accept what I see there, I can never really value it. Worse, I'll live in fear that someone else will see to the core of me and reject me, too.

But that's precisely where the God who birthed us, our

loving Mother God, becomes the mainstay, not the menace of our lives. God knows exactly who we are. God knows our frailty. And God accepts it. And gathers it in. God loves us, not despite it, but because of it, because of the effort it implies and the trust it demands. There is glory in the clay of us. There is beauty in becoming.

There is such a thing as trying too hard. Be easy on yourself. When all is said and done we will still be only human.

You love those who search for truth.
In wisdom, center me, for you know my frailty.
Psalm 51:6

Simplicity

Abbot Mark once said to Abbot Arsenius, "It is good, is it not, to have nothing in our cell that just gives us pleasure? For example, I once knew a brother who had a little wild flower that came up in his cell and he pulled it out by the roots." "Well," said Abbot Arsenius, "that is all right. But each person should act according to her own spiritual way. And if one were not able to get along without the flower, she should plant it again."

SIMPLICITY OF LIFE in a complex and complicated world is marked, I think, by four characteristics. A life is simple if it is honest, if it is unencumbered, if it is open to the ideas of others, if it is serene in the midst of a mindless momentum that verges on the chaotic.

At base, simplicity of life has a great deal more to do with authenticity than it does with things—or else it would be a virtue only for those who had things to forego. Then simplicity would have more to do with classism, with a kind of social play called "voluntary simplicity," than with an attitude of mind that lets us stand in the midst of our world naked and unafraid, sure of soul and unencumbered by the seductiveness of the unnecessary and the cosmetic.

Isn't simplicity really what the ancients called "purity of heart"—that single-minded search for the essence of life rather than for a grasping after its frills, whatever shape those might take in our various worlds? Doesn't simplicity require that we learn how to live a centered life, to "make God our portion," in a world that tears our days, our lives, our psyches into tangled shreds?

Blessed are the pure of heart,
they shall see God.
Matthew 5:8

Spirituality

Once upon a time, as the Master lay dying, the disciples begged him, for their sakes, not to go. "But if I do not go," the Master said, "how will you ever see?" "But what are we not seeing now that we will see when you are gone?" they asked. And the Master said, "All I ever did was sit on the river bank handing out river water. After I'm gone, I trust you will notice the river."

⌒

RELIGION AND SPIRITUALITY are not the same thing. They are, however, commonly confused. "She goes to church every week," we say. "She is a very spiritual person." Or we note that, "He's a staunch member of the parish finance committee. He's a very spiritual person." It's an interesting conjunction of unlike ideas. It's the equivalent of saying, "She's an excellent vocalist. She's been taking lessons for years." There's certainly a connection between taking voice lessons and becoming a professional vocalist, but it's not a necessary one. The truth is that we can go through the motions about something all our lives and never really become what the thing itself is meant to make us.

Religion and spirituality are like that, too. The one, religion, has to do with leading us to an awareness of God. The other, spirituality, has to do with transforming the way we live out that awareness. Sometimes we stop at one and fail to become the other.

It's when we make religion itself our substitute for God that, ironically, our spirits stand to wither or calcify. The Sufi poet Hafiz put it this way:

The
great religions are the
ships.

Poets the life
boats.

Every sane person I know
has jumped
overboard!

That is good for business,
isn't it,
Hafiz?

This is what God asks of you, only this:

to act justly, love tenderly and walk humbly with your God.
Micah 6:8

Stability

A man once dreamed that a great treasure was hidden under a bridge in Vienna. Since he lived in a remote village, the dream seemed absurd to him, and he tried to ignore it. But night after night he had the same dream. Finally he made the long journey to Vienna, where he found the bridge he had dreamed about. Because of the many people who used the bridge, he dared not search for the treasure by day. Besides, a sentry stood close by.

After several days of watching the man stand and regard the bridge, the sentry asked him, "What are you doing here?" Hoping that the sentry would share the treasure with him, the man decided to tell the whole story and ask for help. On hearing the story, the sentry replied, "You are here because of a dream, only a dream? I also had a dream, and I also saw a treasure. This treasure was in a small house in a distant village, hidden under a cellar. But who bothers with dreams?"

In relating his dream, the sentry had accurately described the man's village and house. The man rushed home, dug under his cellar, and found the treasure. "Now I know that I had the treasure all along," he exclaimed. "But I had to travel to Vienna to find it."

THE FIRST INTERNATIONAL TRIP I ever took taught me a lot about staying home. In fact, it brought me face-to-face with one of the essential lessons of life: Excitement can be a very boring thing. The monotony of constant movement, of unending change, of daily discontinuity can wear the spirit down all the time it is stirring it up.

The point is clear: The soul can only wander so far, so long, before it finds itself adrift. Without direction, without purpose, without a sense of security, the insight that comes from immersion in the familiar begins to pale. We lose our way. We find ourselves having to focus on the rudiments of life rather than able to reflect on the purpose of life. We lose touch—even with a sense of ourselves.

The only antidote to drift is stability.

Stability, a sense of home, of being where we belong, gives us, ironically, the luxury to think about more than the mundane. Stability, the ongoing awareness of being securely cemented in something as well as liberated by it, is the caisson that is one of the foundations of human growth.

In God alone there is rest for my soul,
from God alone comes my safety; with God alone
for my rock, my safety, my fortress, I can never fail.
Psalm 62:1-2

Time

A handful of wheat grains was found in the tomb of the ancient Egyptian kings. The grains were five thousand years old. Someone planted the grains and watered them. And, to the amazement of all, the grains came to life and sprouted. After five thousand years!

TIME IS ONE OF THE FEW dimensions of life that has no properties. It is not short or tall, heavy or thin, old or young. It just is. Time has only those qualities that we ourselves give to it.

Time is meant to free us for life; but, instead, time enslaves us. Instead of listening to the people we're with, we keep checking our watches to make sure that we're on time for the person who's coming next. We live with our minds on something else instead of the presence of God in the present. So we miss our children growing up. We miss the middle years of marriage. We miss the calls within us to live life in new ways. We lose time and think we're living. How sad. Be here—now.

Time is sacred. Time is holy. Time is the raw material of the sacramental. Somehow or other we have to understand that this life is our life and the way we spend it is the kind of person we will, in the end, come to be. This life is the only one we have. What a pity to come to the end of it saying, "I could have...I should have... but I didn't."

All our days pass away;
our life is over in a breath.
Psalm 90:9

Wisdom

A certain dervish was respected for his piety and appearance of virtue. Whenever anyone asked him how he had become so holy, he always answered, "I know what is in the Koran." One day he had just given this reply to an inquirer in a coffeehouse when a seeker asked, "Well, what is in the Koran?" "In the Koran," said the dervish, "there are two pressed flowers and a letter from my friend."

I FOUND MYSELF on an island which, eight months before my arrival, a hurricane had tossed upside down. There are huge, gaping spaces all over the island. Where houses and businesses, grand hotels and baronial palm trees once stood, there's now nothing but an empty reminder of the power that is greater than we are.

I wondered what it is that enables people to get up and go on again beyond the disasters of their lives, more sober than before, perhaps, but determined, nevertheless. In each of these devastated areas, in fact, the rebuilding had begun.

Most of all, how is it that each of us, on a smaller scale maybe, but with just the same degree of shock and disorientation and fear go through the catastrophes of our lives and survive? Like this small island, struck head on, what is it that enables us to get up again? The cancer does not stop us from living a full life. The job loss does not leave us in despair. The death in the family does not extinguish our own spirits.

Then last night I began reading a newly published book here that records the personal experiences of each of the survivors. There was a common denominator to almost all of them. One person after another told of carrying their bibles from room to room in the house as the roof over their heads splintered like matchsticks. Just carrying it. Holding it in their hands. Clutching it to their breasts.

And then I understood. These people, too, "know what's in the Koran." They know what gives meaning to life. They have wisdom. They know what's important: "…two pressed flowers and a letter from my friend."

Your word is a lamp to guide my feet
and a light on my path.
Psalm 119:105

Notes

Notes